Reflections

A collection of poems by

Steven P. Taylor

Mark.
Hope you enjoy

1

Reflections

ISBN 978-1-9995988-4-6

Printed by Biddles Books Kings Lynn Norfolk PE32 1SF

2nd edition 2018

....

My thanks to...

My family and friends and all the people who have encouraged me with
this venture, all of whom were mentioned in the first edition of this
volume, which should shortly be available at any good car boot sale.

To the legend Dr. John Cooper Clarke for making poetry cool and
inspiring me way back in the 70s.
and
My Mum and Dad for getting it together and producing me.

And you for reading the book.

Love to all
Steven x

The Author

Steven P. Taylor

Started working as a promoter / compere in the early
Eighties during the start of the new or alternative
comedy scene. He ran the 'Laughingas' comedy clubs with
comedian Phil Cool in various Lancashire venues, working with
new comedians including Jack Dee, Jo Brand and Paul Merton.
After a break of ten years he briefly re-launched
'Laughingas' with the likes of Bolton legends Peter Kay,
Bernard Wrigley, Bob Williamson and Hovis Presley.

During all this name dropping he was writing poetry.
It's only over the last couple of years that he has been performing
poetry at pubs, folk clubs and anywhere that people will listen.
He was educated at Elton Primary school, and then The Derby
School in Bury, where he learned most of the swear words
included in this book, and how to blow smoke rings.
He lives in Ramsbottom and has a leaking kitchen roof.

The Poems

Reflections

The selection of poems / songs in this book were mainly
written over the last three years and reflect childhood and growing
up, social comment, love, humour and general observations.
This second edition contains a few alterations and updates.

Contact

Email   stevetaylorok@aol.com

Facebook   Steven P. Taylor — Poetry

Web site   www.stevenptaylorpoetry.com

Tel   07764 573483

Reviews / Comments

"When he (Steven) asked me to check out this book of his work and give him some feedback. I must say I was astonished and impressed by how carefully crafted these poems are, comedic and serious alike.
As well as being clever and funny, they've also been given that special tender touch. If I wasn't now retired from writing I might even be slightly jealous".

Phil Cool (comedian, writer)

....

".... a bloody good writer.' When you read a piece and think "Well, that's very true" or "Those are my views exactly" it can be hard to appreciate the work that's gone into it because that's just how YOU would have expressed it. If you could, that is. Have fun reading them - I know I certainly did".

Bernard Wrigley (writer, comedian, poet, actor, musician)

....

" Steven's poems hold a mirror up to everyday life. They're insightful, thought provoking and funny. And there's more - I defy you not to tap your foot when you're reciting some of them out loud"

Jimmy Cricket (comedian)

....

"My old mate Steven has written his first book of poetry and it's cracking. Like the secret love child of John Cooper Clarke and Pam Ayres, he muses with warmth and wit on his life, loves and Lancashire. With each verse, the bartender turned tender bard, gradually reveals himself, like his 'girl on the peanut card', and the result is a great read, from a good lad".

Mark Hurst /Mark Miwurdz (comedian, poet, writer)

....

".....his prose is impassioned, intellectual, ethereal, and funny..... "

Austin Knight (comedian)

....

".....A funny man and a proper gent who writes proper poems."

Dave Cohen (comedian, writer- Have I Got News For You, Spittin- Image, Horrible Histories)

....

."..very enjoyable and well written"

Mark Potter (guitarist/writer—Elbow)

Contents

Contents

Reflections

Reflections
Recollections
Memories of my past.
Crave brave times
Grave rave times
Disappear so fast.

Like all the days
Are holidays
When I can reflect.
No deal I feel
That spiel's not real
Seen in retrospect.

Youth aching
Heart breaking
We all had a blast.
Cool school days
Fuel cruel ways
Knew it couldn't last.

Middle age
Comes with rage
Brings in confusion.
Learn and earn
Yearn time will turn
More disillusion.

Formative years
Laughs and tears
Good for a little while.
Love and fashion
Rationed passion
Always in the style.

Keep looking back
Defend attack
That's your predilection.
Times glad you had
Some mad some sad
All in the reflection.

Wouldn't it be better?

If cherries didn't have stones
If fish didn't have bones.
If our lives had action replays
If we hadn't had 70s DJs.
If I could get fit without being active
If Kate Moss found me attractive.
If Sinatra were here to croon
If Posh Spice could hold a tune.
If people didn't hold grudges
If The X Factor didn't have tosser judges.
If fast food could be delicious
Good for you and nutritious.
If snooker commentators lost their banality
And somehow found personality.
If animals weren't kept in a cage
If Michael McIntyre could fall off the stage.

Wouldn't it be better?

If MPs weren't so sinister
If Joey Essex could be Prime Minister.
If restaurants had better lighting
If cricket could be exciting.
If you could constantly have good health
If the ironing would do itself.
If we never ever had to queue
If there'd never been the pop group Blue.
If the vulnerable could be assisted
If Gary Glitter had never existed.
If they pensioned off Take That
If Justin Bieber wasn't such a twat.
If there wasn't fear inside us
If my house didn't have spiders.
If I could play a great Hammond Organ
If I could repeatedly punch Piers Morgan.

Wouldn't it be better?

If holidays were longer
If the whole world did a conga.
If we had Oscar Wilde and Noel Coward
Instead of Russell Kane and Russell Howard.
If boxing still had big Frank
Mohammad Ali and Chris Eubank.
If age didn't come with pain
If I could be sixteen again.
If it didn't constantly rain
If Portillo got hit by his train.
If I'd thought twice before getting wed
If I could have been better in bed.
If we could find a solution
To the sea and ocean pollution.
If they were quicker on roads with grit
If the council weren't so full of shit.

Wouldn't it be better?

If young people would read more books
And stop being obsessed with their looks.
And realise that health is
Not just looking good on selfies.
If trains would arrive on time
And didn't blame 'leaves on the line'.
If older people could stay wiser
If God forgot to invent Alzheimer's.
If I'd have worked harder at school
Instead of just playing the fool.
If dogs could clean their own mess
If Gyles Brandreth would speak less.
If we never had Trick or Treat again
If Christmas came just one in ten.
If we could all retain our youth
If Tony Blair could tell the truth.

Wouldn't it be better?

If people didn't have bad dreams
If Milk Tray didn't have coffee creams.
If there were no wasps just bees
If chocolate bars grew on trees.
If the government gave us all free beer
If TV magicians would all disappear.
If the summers could be sunnier
If this poem could be funnier.
If traffic wardens would give and take
And negotiate for goodness sake.
If Joanna Lumley got all flirty
And started talking dirty.

Wouldn't it be better?

If life stopped being too taxing
And more time was spent relaxing.
If it was safe to walk in the park
Or the streets on your own after dark.
If people didn't need to carry knives
If more value was put on lives.
If communities were educated
To mix and not be segregated.
If birds were allowed to fly freely
If the blind could one day see clearly.
If everyone gives what they can
If man could be humane to man.
If starvation was all in the past
If peace and love could last.
If all Gods were rolled into one
So hatred and violence were gone.

Wouldn't it be better?
Wouldn't it be better?
It would be better.

The media create mediocrity

The media create mediocrity
Creativeness stifled and held
Forward thinking
Is quickly sinking
Like a flourishing sapling felled.

So what's the point of imagination
The future left in the past
Avant-garde
Is as good as barred
So nothing of value can last.

Mainstream takes over the fringes
Populist only comes through
Creative brain
On a higher plain
Redundant now nothing to do.

If life had always been this way
Lucy hadn't been in the sky
And Banksy's shouts
Were painted out
And Munch's scream, but a cry.

Never let mediocrity prosper
For thought is the heart of the start.
And ignore the mundane
As there is the blame
Bring reprise not demise to the arts.

He split his time between Antarctic and Arctic
He chose whichever was colder
His friends thought he was crazy
His doctor diagnosed bipolar.

Moving on.

What's going on, there's no pots in the sink?
The fridge is full, no one's taken my drink.
The cushions aren't piled up or thrown on the floor,
There's no mass of shoes out blocking the door.
Something's not right here, there's trouble afoot,
It's all looking neat so there must be a but.
The linen basket has got nothing in,
There's no piles of empties filling the bin.
There's no sign around of specialist diet,
In fact things have gone suspiciously quiet.
Oh now I remember the cause of all this,
And I waved her off with a tear and kiss.
I'll cope I know with this adversity,
The Teenager is at University.

A life changing event and I'll have to cope,
It won't be easy but I'll manage I hope.
I've still got my memories while she's away,
I'll certainly think about her every day.
She's out in the big world, I'll not see her soon,
I wonder how much I can get for her room.

I'm having a 'lie in'

I'm having a 'lie in' my bed,
Getting up fills me with dread,
I just despise,
An early rise,
I love to doze instead.

I'm really not ready to play,
I much prefer it this way,
I'll carry on zzzedding,
While wrapped up in bedding,
I just wanna stay here all day.

It's the way I'm genetically built,
Don't try to make me feel guilt,
I like it alone,
Here in the zone,
Just me and my bloody big quilt.

So leave me I'm staying right here,
I couldn't make it more clear,
You go off together,
In this nasty weather,
You'll not get me out, no fear.

I'm avoiding the wind and the showers,
Off you go to your big office towers,
Your appointments need keeping,
While I stay here sleeping,
For at least a couple more hours.

Lovely name for a town

Not every town has idyllic names, that sound like parts of heaven.
There's Great Cockup and Lickey End, and Crapstone down in Devon.

There's Little Bushey, Sandy Balls and Horny Man in Kent.
Shitlingthorpe in Yorkshire, or even Cwm in Gwent.

Take a look at Nob End, where you're more than a number.
Or get yourself out east coast, to Fudgepack upon Humber.

Take a trip to Dorset, the place is named from hell.
With Shitterton and Scratchy Bottom and the town of Shaggs as well.

There's lots of places to go and stroll, round villages towns and parks.
There's Dicksmount, Cockshot and Brown Willy, Snatchup and Fanny Barks.

If that's not enough try Rimswell, Toss Side or Titty Ho.
But if you take a trip Upper Chute, be careful how you go.

You may like Happy Bottom, or Willey or Bell End.
But personally I enjoyed Lickar Moor, with a very special friend.

It's just as bad in Scotland with, Broken Wind and Fannyfield.
Backsides, Dick Court and Tarty, they're the real deal.

So just be happy with where you live, in your big house or your flat.
Cos you could live up in the Orkneys, in a little town called Twatt.

The Traffic Warden

He seems a normal type of guy
Going his own way.
But it's his life's raison d'être
To ruin someone's day.

You cannot say a word to him
Or he gets all farty smarty.
Looking like Blakey from On The Buses
Or a member of a fascist party.

With his pseudo Nazi uniform
Decisions of finality.
His ultra hi-viz jacket
And lo-viz personality.

I tried to reason with him
But he's having none of that.
As he hands over my ticket
The heartless jobsworth twat.

He could have some humanity
Hang on just a bit.
I was only one minute over
The power mad little shit.

So I take my ticket with me
Pay the bloody fine.
Perhaps I'll be more punctual
At any future time.

Suppose someone has to do that job
It's one man or another.
But what really pisses me off
Is that guy was my brother.

Remember

A paper flower on your lapel,
Acknowledging all those who fell,
Reflect on the eleventh hour,
Significance of that red flower.

Our minds can't take the sheer thought,
Futility of wars they fought,
Of all the horrors they endured,
Yet future peace can't be assured.

The leaders at The Cenotaph,
Caring? No don't make me laugh,
Hypocritically stand by,
Then send more young men out to die.

No one will learn and you can bet,
History will but show regret,
We can only pay our debt,
They laid their lives, 'Lest we forget'.

Go for it

You're searching for a pot of gold before you've even seen a rainbow
You want to fly a kite before you've even felt the wind blow
You're obviously determined and what the hell do I know
So do your worst, expand your mind, good luck wherever you go.

You want to do a marathon before you've learnt to walk
You want to recite Shakespeare before you've learned to talk
You try to eat with chopsticks you can hardly use a fork
You've never gone further than Bolton, yet you're aiming for New York.

So live your life the way you like, who am I to interfere?
You never rode a motor bike yet you've got all the gear
Your plans are surely laudable and I'm being quite sincere
But if it all comes crashing in you know I'll still be waiting here.

I'm only trying to help you, I don't want to see you fall
Aim big there's nothing wrong with that but first you must start small
Having conversation with you is like talking to a wall
You have no sense of fear because you have no sense at all.

You have your own ambitions got to have a try
Agreed if you do nothing the world will pass you by
But you must take it sensibly not just pie in the sky
You have to do what's right for you, so do so, do or die.

It's nice to be insignificant

It's nice to be insignificant
It's good to blend into the pack
It's comforting to look at folk
Knowing they won't look back

As people wander past me
It's like I wasn't there
If they never saw me in their life
I'm sure they wouldn't care

I've got one of those faces
It's just the way it goes
That no one recognises and
No one even knows

I like to be mister nobody
Getting on with what I can
Ghost my way through life
Like the invisible man

Yes it's good to be insignificant
Get on with my day to day
I'm happy being unimportant
And living my own special way

When you blend in to the background
It can be rather nice
It's amazing what you get away with
When nobody looks twice

So leave me in my little world
As you all continue further
With your petty conforming lives
While I get away with murder.

Magaluf

English breakfast
Fish and chips
Sangria and
Skinny dips
Airport books
To read by day
DaVinci Code
Shades of Grey
Jagerbombs
Lined up queuing
Down the side streets
Drinkers spewing
Multi story
Concrete blocks
Jesus boots and
Pulled up socks
Itsi bitsi
Teeny weeny
Hideous green
Borat mankini
Holiday girls
Looking curvy
Holiday reps
Staring pervy
Sunbeds sardined
Toe to toe
Packed in tight
Nowhere to go
Parasol, deckchair
All for letting
Accommodating
Bodies sweating

Two for one bars
Flamenco guitars
Pycho drunk nutters
Face down in gutters
Cheap hotels
Curious smells
Overnight chums
New teenage mums
On the corner
Substance buying
Eyes are gone
High and flying
Stag nights
Bar fights
Curry bites
Screaming shites
Dancing Lambada
Piña colada
Crap tribute singers
Middle ages swingers
Topless lassies
Bottomless glasses
Bum bags
Lads mags
Groping hands
One night stands
Inappropriate flirts
Football shirts
Pushy bouncers
Noisy Scousers
Littered streets
Dirty sheets

Plastic glasses
Wobbling asses
Steroid muscles
Side street hustles
Unflushable loos
Back street tattoos
Beer bellies
Satellite tellies
Braided hair
Ambre Solaire
Red lamps
Tramp stamps
Saggy white skin
Watered down gin
Old has beens
Vivid scenes
Sunburnt backs
Builder's cracks
Drinking trips
On pirate ships
18/30
Dirty dirty
Union flags
Usual slags
Night strippers
Day trippers

I can't get enough
All this stuff
Take be back
To Magaluf

Comes with age

While walking through the shops,
Or running for a bus .
While reading in a library,
Not wanting any fuss.

Whether finishing a day at work,
Or even when you're starting.
All these are times we are prone to,
Involuntary farting.

It's not our fault, it's age,
Like the pumping of the heart.
Like strange hot sweats and rage,
The involuntary fart.

As you watch your favourite TV,
Football, snooker or the darts.
You can punctuate the commentary,
With involuntary farts.

During normal body functions,
A sneeze or just a cough.
May also cause you to,
Accidentally rip one off.

When you see a friend approaching,
And you wave and give a shout.
You can bet that as you catch their eye,
You'll launch another out.

On a Sunday with your priest,
Confessing what you've sinned.
He'll give you far more penance for,
An unexpected break of wind.

This unfortunate affliction,
And you can surely call it that.
Can often be disguised,
By blaming on the cat.

So listen when I tell ,
These wise words I'm imparting.
For you too will get the curse,
Of involuntary farting.

Daytime TV

Daytime TV drives me insane,
It's drab and moronic and killing my brain.
There's nothing there to raise a smile,
Just a series of lowlifes on Jeremy Kyle.
Sat on settee in tracky and vest,
Waiting for results of paternity test.
There's game shows where you need to be skilful and thrifty,
That demand an IQ approaching 50.
This morning will teach you about food, weight and slimming,
Then try your hardest to sit through Loose Women.
Judge Rinder resides with law suits to bring,
In his camp court where sarcasm is king.
There's numerous programmes on antiques to buy,
With some pompous prick with a spotted bow tie.
Countdown's essential viewing for nerds,
I just hope and pray for unplanned rude words.
The afternoon soaps about doctors and vets,
With piss poor acting and wobbly sets.
There's adverts for pensions and PPI buying,
And a free Parker pen when you make plans for dying.
This daytime TV really isn't for me,
I'll have to prise myself off the settee.
So I'd better get up and work for a while,
Or I'll end up with that lot on Jeremy Kyle.

Before the dawn

A street light flickers, the early morning
Deserted roads before the dawning.

A solitary figure stealing away
From a lighted room at break of day
The need of a friend, a glance up above
Silhouette at the window, been shopping for love
An urge, a desire, a call for assistance
A future of clouds, artificial existence.

The dew on the park, haze over the lake
And newspaper sleepers begin to awake
From four poster benches with blankets of frost
And wine in the gutter, another is lost.

The elegant gent a wager is fed
Dejection, self pity, lost all on the red
Escape from a race it's a gamble on chance
Obsession, addiction a pledge of romance.

The street light dims, daybreak arrives
Bustling commuters continue their lives
Blind to events, clandestine deeds
Of human thoughts and human needs.

I love you

I love you for your kindness
Your never ending giving
I love just being here with you
You make my life worth living.

I love you cos you're beautiful
I love you cos you're funny
But most of all I love you because
You've got stacks of money.

Hazel

She's the girl boys want to see,
She's the girl girls want to be,
She was a wonderful friend to me,
We love you Hazel.

She would light up any room,
She'd take away any gloom,
She could never come around too soon,
We love you Hazel.

Her image was always cool,
With fashion she had no rule,
She sparkled like a jewel,
We love you Hazel.

I can picture her today,
As she slowly walked away,
In shorts and red beret,
We love you Hazel.

Even though you can't be here,
The memories are clear,
We love you very dear,
We love you Hazel.

xx

Jeans

Why can't I buy a pair of jeans,
A normal pair that fits
Not super skinny denim tights,
That strangulate my bits.

I haven't got the legs for it,
I'm not tall and slim,
These jeans are meant for youngsters,
With physiques far more trim.

What can I do about it?
There's got to be an answer,
I can't go walking round,
Looking like a ballet dancer.

Oh there is a looser type of jean,
Though if it suits I doubt,
The proper way to wear these,
Is with whole arse hanging out.

The selection of jeans I have,
Puts me in quite a rage,
I'm still a human being with needs,
If sadly middle aged.

I could go for the Clarkson look,
But I really don't want that,
A look that has rightly been described,
As dressing like a twat!

So I'll plod on unfashionably,
My style won't win awards,
At least I don't wear chinos,
Or God protect me, cords.

Out of season

Open stretch of beach deserted and stark,
Threatening waters cold and dark.
Rolling black waves crashing with force,
Taking away all in its course.
Windswept dog walkers braving the storm,
Wrapped in waterproofs try to keep warm.
Lonesome homeless don't fancy his chances,
Curled in the shadows while storm cloud dances.
Donkeys retired for a winter rest,
From a season of pleasing and doing their best.
Shuttered up shops no cockles today,
No kiss me quick hats, all packed away.
The future the past what can they be?
Who knows, there's no sign of gypsy Rosa Lee.
Unseasonal emptiness all you can see,
Barely a cafe for a quick cup of tea.
There's a weather beaten face casting out to sea,
With just a rod and line for company.
He'll stay there all day with hopes and a wish,
Of returning home with a full net of fish.
The rain pours and floods the names of the stars,
That stare up to the tower and the once thriving bars.
Stall holders long done their final cashing,
Leave Victorian piers to a winter thrashing.
The seasons may change the deck chairs all gone,
But the real work now has only begun.
Closed down roller coasters worldly famed,
Silhouetted on pleasure beach, ironically named.
With summer holiday tourists parted,
The plans for next year have already started.
Wind from the Irish Sea blowing wild,
Bringing winter beauty all over the Fylde.
We love it so and that's the reason,
We'll be there in or out of season.

It's my day today

It's my day today
Time is ticking away
Meeting at seven
My girl from heaven
Smartly dressed
Need to impress
Cant be late
My special date
It's after 7.10
Check the door again
At the station bar
She's not travelling far
But no one is here
I'll have one more beer
I've waited for an hour
For the girl with a flower
And I don't know
If she will show
She's very late
It's after 8
She's not coming I fear
Just have another beer
Helps time pass away
It's not my day today.

Don't send me to IKEA

Don't send me to IKEA
It's the one place that I fear
It's a labyrinth of horror
Ending up in nowt but sorrow

Don't send me to IKEA
I've really no idea
I've only ever found
I can't find my way around

Don't send me to IKEA
It doesn't bring me cheer
I only went for a head for my shower
Ended up walking round for an hour

Don't send me to IKEA
I cannot persevere
The time I have is shite there
It's a self assembly nightmare

Don't send me to IKEA
I'd rather go to North Korea
Cos there they are more stable
Than a dodgy coffee table

Don't send me to IKEA
My mother made it clear
I'll only do the same as she did
Buy things I didn't know I needed

Don't send me to IKEA
Their food is really queer
My good appetite quickly falls
With those dubious meat balls

Don't send me to IKEA
I'm being quite sincere
There are far better things to do
Along the M62.

Don't send me to IKEA
It's not a good idea
I won't have a good time
I'll do nothing but whine

Don't send me to IKEA
They don't have full packs of gear
There's always massive queues
To buy products lacking screws
The staff don't even know
Their arse from their elbow
You're waiting there for hours
For a bunch of plastic flowers
When you look at your bill
You'll understand nil
It's the shop from hell I fear
Please.....Don't send me to IKEA !

The you that I first knew.

Sailing through a tempest of emotion
An avalanche of pain, is what I do
Trying to find my way through this confusion
I want to find the you that I first knew.

I've seen it here and there in too brief glances
Need to get closer for a better view
I clearly hold on to what our romance is
Can't wait to find the you that I first knew.

Remembering the times we had such great fun
And they'll be back I promise that is true
It's a case of walking fore we try to run
As I rediscover the you that I first knew.

I'm with you all the time if things are rough
I'll guide and help you all the way through
And always in my mind when times are tough
Is getting back the you that I first knew.

And soon we will make it to the other side
We'll make it together me and you
And I'll be there with tons of love and pride
As I'm back with the you that I first knew.

That summer day

Just the two of us
no one around
Birds and sea
made the only sound

We walked the beach
hand in hand
Wrote our names
in the sand

Lay there with you
by my side
Making love in
the ebbing tide

The waves roll
crystal clear
Making our
names disappear

But the tides
could never erase
Our memories
of those days.

The star who never was

He thinks he is a Rolling Stone
The car he drives, he doesn't own
He's frightened stiff to be alone
He's the star who never was.

His clothes, he's had since '75
A rusting Lambretta on his drive
A hope to bring his dreams alive
The star who never was.

A leather jacket angel wings
Patches, badges, chains and things
But punters scarper if he sings
The star who never was.

He's there at the open mic night
He stands with his pint of snake bite
If he could he'd stay there all night
The star who never was.

His greying beard is full of food
He calls everyone 'man' or 'dude'
He's a tattoo of something very rude
The star who never was.

A permanent fixture at the bar
Talking to those near or far
Of how he nearly was a star
The star who never was.

He never ever dresses dowdy
You'll never find him being rowdy
Wears his shades even when it's cloudy
The star who never was.

Buy him a double rum and Coke
He'll tell you his best smutty joke
Then sneak out for a herbal smoke
The star who never was.

He's a mod a rocker and any other
A hippy or even a soul brother
Has his pint and then it's home to mother
For the star who never was.

His Lennon shades perch on the nose
Patchouli oil drench his clothes
He stands out everywhere he goes
The star who never was.

When trying to sing he just gets jeered
Some people think he's rather weird
He dabs boot polish on his beard
The star who never was.

So back to mums and off to bed
With dreams still running through his head
Of if he'd been Robert Plant instead
Of a star who never was.

Same old town

Shopping centres taken over,
North of Scotland down to Dover
Only big boys have a shout
Independents all priced out
Every town looks like the other
Nothing new now to discover
Trudging up and down the street
Aching legs and aching feet
Ending up in same old joint
What's the reason what's the point
Morning drinkers every time
Wetherspoons at the crack of 9
Pound shop, pawn shop, bookies too
Have a pint then a tattoo
Same shop names in every street
Originality obsolete
No variety what's the game
Every towns the bleeding same
Shitty people shitty places
Same old bloody shitty faces
Special dinner, you'll be lucky
Fatty greasy old Kentucky.
There's no choice fried chicken legs
Cold McNuggets, fuckin Gregg's
You may as well stay where you are
No need to travel very far
Uniformity that's the game
Cos everywhere's the bloody same.

The day Johnny said 'rude word'

The day Johnny said 'rude word'
And Grundy asked for more
The boys joined in whole heartedly
That opened up the door.

And all the kids said 'oh yes
This is what we need
This is what we're all about
Now he's taken the lead'.

So we all bought old guitars
Or sets of battered drums
And found a quiet cellar
With all like minded chums.

We didn't have much talent
But attitude overflowed
With vigorous raw energy
And that was what we showed.

There we all then were
With anger and much to say
Thanks to Johnny's 'rude word'
We changed the world that day.

New Years Eve

This New Years Eve
I'll thank God above
For giving me friends
and giving me love

This New Year's Eve
I'll have a safe time
Maybe one beer or
a small glass of wine

This New Year's Eve
I'll try not to spoil it
Ending the night
Face down in the toilet .

Dining out

Went out to eat posh the other day,
Nouvelle cuisine they say is the way.
The restaurant where the connoisseur goes,
Where the waiter looks at you down his nose.
The portions were so terribly small,
There was hardly any food there at all.
I didn't complain I just stayed quiet,
Maybe they thought I needed to diet.
I said waiter this bowl is slightly wet,
He said that's your soup, I thought, cheeky get.
I didn't want to seem to overstate,
But there was room for another meal on my plate.
The rare steak I ordered was cooked so blue,
I thought for a minute I heard it moo.
Food was dribbled drizzled and splashed,
There were no potatoes not boiled, chipped or mashed.
No cabbage or carrots, sprouts, peas or swede,
Just kale and ochre, mange tout and seaweed.
The portions so skimpy although they look neat,
Are more like a painting than something to eat.
It was quite an experience I have to say,
Seems the less food you get, the more you pay.
So I paid up the bill after getting a loan,
And called at the chippy on the way home.

An Englishman's home is..........(was)

Another business another house,
More innocents attacked,
Intimacy infiltrated,
Abused obscenely hacked.
Alarm is ringing on deaf ears,
No one bats an eye,
No cops feet to beat the street,
Oblivious passers by.
Anytime of day or night,
Never knowing when it may come,
A lovingly built up place to call home,
Contaminated by scum.
No police presence on our streets,
No security of any kind,
How do we sleep safe at night in our beds,
When we have no peace of mind.
When robbery and violence are everyday things,
No deterrent is set for the crimes,
Community service is all they expect,
In these unjust and worrying times.
A state that's seeming not to care,
Where crime figure record booms,
And safety of public is wholly ignored,
As a lawless society looms.
So where does it end who is to blame,
Is it Blair is it Thatcher or May,
Or has it always just been the same,
Will stay this day way in dismay.
And life goes on, take your chance,
A rat race, run day to day,
There are those who work hard for their families,
And those vile who'll take it away.

Drinks to...

Drinks to remember
And drinks to forget
Drinks for the good times
And drinks to regret

Drinks to the 'could be'
May go on forever
And drinks to what wanted
But knew they could never

So drink to the one girl
That will stop me from sinking
You know that she's not there
So drink to 'keep drinking'

The English Chippy

On every sea front in England's fair land,
As familiar to all as the sea and the sand,
Whatever you're doing the one place to stop,
The pride of the nation, the fish and chip shop.
A newspaper takeaway, great thing to do,
Or sat in the cafe and served with a brew,
Freshly prepared, there's no frozen stuff here,
An assortment of dishes from far and from near.
Displayed in its glory a treat for the eyes,
An abundance of fritters, puddings and pies,
Fresh from the seas all there for the take,
A bounty of cod, haddock and hake.
A truly wondrous seafood selection,
In crispy batter fried to perfection,
A list of fresh pies readily regaled,
From chicken or cheese to steak and ale.
There's Heinz baked beans or mushy peas,
Gastronomic delight and sure to please,
A jumbo sausage plain or battered,
Anyway you like it doesn't matter.
Ever evolving and ready to please,
Keep the kids happy with chips and cheese,
The original fast food for those in a hurry,
You can't beat a big plate of fish chips and curry.

So forget your fancy restaurants with their hummus and their
dips,
There's nothing in this world tops English fish and chips.

Pale Legs

I need a summer holiday,
I need it more than most,
I'm looking all anaemic,
I'm looking like a ghost.

I need to look like David Dickinson,
Or others of that ilk,
My poor legs currently look like,
A couple of pints of milk.

I need those ultra violet rays,
I've gotta have some sun,
And be looking bronzed all over,
Well, all except me bum.

Strutting tanned along the beach,
Looking cool and groovy,
As I wade out of the sea in Speedo's,
Like a scene from a James Bond movie.

So you see I like to have a tan,
As much as I am able,
And have legs like a Spanish hunk,
Or at least a mahogany table.

Loneliness

Loneliness
A state of play
A state of mind
A time of day
A silent place
A ghostly tomb
A market place
A crowded room
The quiet of dark
A party of fun
The noise in the park
A table for one.

Love Life

Take your hopes and dreams and run with them,
Your thoughts and your ideas, have fun with them.
Don't hear those needless protests that they shout,
Their unfounded suspicions and their doubts.
For these will only serve to hold you back,
Take a more positive plan of attack.
When after all this life is yours alone,
And independently your mind has grown.
So go with all your plans and all your dreams,
It won't be as complex as it first seems.
The time and opportunity is here,
And now seems propitious and clear.
Embark on this a journey of your youth,
Track down suppressed and vaguely hidden truth.
Life's lessons there start to become unfurled,
Life, the university of the world.
Don't seek contentment just achieved by stealth,
The love you yearn is right there in yourself.

Love yourself
Love life.

I don't belong

There's a black stage
A spotlight
Fright light
A space
My space
On the face
Tension
Apprehension
Maybe regret
A bead of sweat
Anticipation
Trepidation
Shaking
Quaking
It's time
I hear my name
It's a muffled sound
Drowned
By pounding heart
From the start
That feeling revealing
Fear
Always here
As the time goes by
Why, why, why
Always my choice
Shaking voice
Like the first time
And so
And so I go
Like every time

Could go either way
Today
More doubts
Distant shouts
What's it all about
It's insane
Never again
Never
Ever
Ah well
What the hell
Here we go
There are laughs
Odd gaffs
There are tears
Even cheers
It's ok.....
.....this time
It works
It's fine
Who knew?
Few
I knew (phew)
I'll be back
Next time
Every time
It's what it's about
Never in doubt
Can't be wrong
It's where I belong

Beautiful boy.

Beautiful boy.
You bring a ray of sunshine to my day.
I'll stand for hours on end and watch you play.
Never being quite sure what to say.
The greatest thing to see,
Is when you smile at me,
Beautiful boy.

Beautiful boy.
A great bundle of energy abound.
Can't fail to cheer me up when you're around.
You shout into my mind without a sound.
May you forever be,
A light that shines in me,
Beautiful boy.

Beautiful boy.
Enduring all the hardships thrown at you.
Smiling in your play and coming through.
Shows intensive strength the way you do.
I say with all my heart,
I love playing my small part,
Beautiful boy.

Beautiful boy.
There's joy to be found just everywhere.
I can't get enough of the times we share.
You can bet your life that I really care.
All of your being,
That I am seeing,
A beautiful boy.

A walk in the Lakes

As the mist like a carpet rolls over the fell,
And the strong icy wind cuts in you like hell,
It's the North it's the Lakes it's so easy to tell,
And you know that you've never been feeling this well.

Its beauty, it's rugged it's hazy it's clear,
It brings such excitement yet also much fear,
It brings to the eye more than many a tear,
If there's anywhere I want to be then it's here.

It's a contradiction all seasons in one,
The sun burns your neck and then there is none,
A lightning flash blink your eyes and it's gone,
It's just you and the elements feeling as one.

There's no scenery like it in many a land,
You talk to the locals they'll tell you "it's grand",
There's everyone happy to lend you a hand,
In a different class to your bland sea and sand.

A life

A life
A miracle
So beautiful
So pure,

A love
Unrivalled
Not knowing
Unsure,

A task ?
A monument
Great joy
An elation,

No task
A yearning
A calling
Vocation,

To learn
And to grow
From innocence
And purity,

To look
And to find
My love and
Security.

All alone together.

Late night in the city
Two people all alone
Nowhere else to go now
So far away from home

Nightclub fever gripping
No time left here to save
It's the moonlight calling
From beyond the rave

The situation here
Two people with one mind
Inevitable choice
To share love of a kind

Hang the consequences
Disregard whoever
Tonight we choose to spend
All alone, together.

Cyber friends

Why should I talk to you when I've got my phone,
I'd really much rather be alone,
On here I can have a right good moan,
Yes it's far better being on my own.

So I'd rather spend time alone you bet,
And join the Twitter and Facebook set,
That's the solitude I want and yet,
I spend the time seeing how many friends I can get.

So are cyber friends any better than real?
They don't come to your place scrounging a meal,
You can turn them off whenever you feel,
The situation to me seems quite ideal.

But cyber friends for all their might,
Can't be there to hold me tight,
Reassure me when I get a fright,
Lie beside me all the night.

So perhaps I should try to spend the day,
Interacting with friends at work and play,
Technology has its place but hey,
Maybe why not just once, put my phone away.

Living the dream

Plotting, scheming, fantasizing, dreaming
Bound up in your world of chance
Wishing hoping hardly ever coping
Gambling too much on romance.

Chasing, pushing, adrenalin rushing
Flirting with substances new
Offers tempting, still experimenting
Just another high to do.

Privately promiscuous, sexually ambiguous
Hedonistic to extreme
There are no barriers, worry not the carriers
They don't fit into your scheme.

Uppers and downers, all over towners
Shadow down an alleyway
Far from the gazing spaced out amazing
Life abusing way to pay.

Biblical confessors, natural transgressors
Hidden in full view of all
Trusting confusion lead by delusion
Stepping to so surely fall.

And so that's the choice made, deed done and price paid
So be it if that is your will
But one day I will bet, you'll see and you'll regret
When paying the ultimate bill.

Party Girl (Live to live)

Party girl
Lost in your party world
The nights no sleeping
The days laid weeping
Your life's in a whirl.

Times like these
Keep me all night, pleased
We have no secrets
No time for regrets
The moment seized.

The man comes by
Heaven sent from the sky?
Sure good for trading
Reality fading
Just one more high.

Flying.
All of life's a game when she's
flying.
Nothing seems the same till she's
crying.
Living with the shame again, she's
crying.
Feeling all the blame again, she's down.

Party fun
Oh can't it still go on
Experience tasting
Life is wasting
My special one.

All night long
Don't tell me this is wrong
You do your thing
Just let me sing
This is my song.

You were the one
Darkness now where your light shone
Our world is sober
The party's over
Our love is gone.

Flying.
All of life's a game when she's
flying.
Nothing seems the same till she's
crying.
Living with the shame again, she's
crying.
Feeling all the blame again, she's down.

And now my world
Is missing one sparkling pearl
Love to give
Live to live
My party girl.

The Bouncer!

He's at the gym everyday,
Works out hard and trains,
He's more muscles than you can imagine,
Certainly more than brains.

He stands before the mirror,
And sees a real new man,
All plucked and shaved and trimmed,
With an orangey spray tan.

He works the doors at weekends,
The power that he dreams,
The ultimate decision maker,
'You can't come in, in jeans'.

Refers to girls as love and babe,
Or sweetheart or chick,
And blokes as pal and cock and mate,
He really is a prick.

Standing there like he is God's gift,
Picking on anyone small,
Thinks he's someone special,
He's a bully boy that's all.

He wears a tight fit dinner suit,
Hair greased back all flat ,
He thinks he looks the business,
I think he looks a twat.

But he has his little place in life,
To supervise the door,
And show off his bulging muscles,
And IQ of twenty four.

A Chance Meeting

Hey, good to see you, it's been ages, hope you've been ok,
Must be ten years since we both went our own separate way,
What's been happening with you, you're still looking really good,
You must be doing well. Well you know I always said you would.

The times we had,
They weren't half bad,
When we were young.

I remember you used to say you thought I was really funny,
Hey, did you marry that guy, you know. The one with all the money,
And did it buy you all the happiness to make you really live,
I could not compete with that, cos love was all I could give.

We all were learning,
With feelings yearning,
When we were young.

So you're back now after all those many happy years,
Won't you tell me, what's the reason then, for all those tears,
Your friends said to me that you were not really coping,
And that your life now, wasn't all that you had been hoping.

And more time passes,
Through rose tint glasses,
When we were young.

Well you know I waited for you for such a long time,
Thinking one day you'd come back and maybe be mine,
There's only so long you can hold out and wait,
I finally moved on and things turned out great.

You know you'll find,
Don't look behind,
When we were young.

Do I want a drink? .....oh that was back in another life,
These are my children, and that lady she's my wife,
So whatever you may hope for whatever you may pray,
You've got to go with your heart and just live for the day.

There are many ways,
To remember the days,
When we were young.

Selfie

Look at me.

Tilt your head and form a half smile with your eyes.

Can't you see.

Takes a lot of pure skill to fake surprise.

Smile again.

It's the one thing now left in my life that's healthy.

One to ten.

It's not a complete day without my host of selfies.

There you go again,
You're looking so good,
You checked so often that,
You knew that you would.
Images and filters,
Flash off flash on,
Any chance of a bad shot,
Are pretty much gone.

It's selfie time hooray,
Today's narcissist way.

Enigma ?

I never know how you're feeling,
There's never a sign that's revealing,

You don't panic when in a hurry,
And never show any signs of worry,

And when you're sad and feeling down,
You never even show a frown,

Expressions are never ever erratic,
You're face remains totally static,

They say that your look is enigmatic,
But I know you're a Botox fanatic.

I just break hearts

I just break hearts
It's what I do
So don't expect much
I can't give it you
Like a bee from flower
To flower I fly
I don't have wild dreams,
No pie in the sky
Don't have time to
Get used to your face
And never stay long
In any one place
Don't read into my mind
I'll be gone in a while
To love and to linger
Is just not my style
I don't get attached
Just flirt and have fun
And love's not my word
It's a time now to run.
Don't think that's a tear
Its dirt in my eye
I don't do emotion
Don't know how to cry
I just break hearts
It's what I do
So don't you go thinking
That I fell for you
You can go off now
And make your new start
I think I've just found
One more broken heart.

Wherever you go.

Whether on the Champs Elysees,
Or at the Colosseum,
On the Bridge of Sighs,
You're guaranteed to see him.

Standing at the Sydney Opera House,
Or sunset at the end of day,
In front of the Taj Mahal,
You can bet he'll be in your way.

At the Brandenburg gate,
Or Checkpoint Charlie,
In Kingston town,
At the house of Bob Marley.

At Aintree for The National,
Or Silverstone's curves,
In front of you at Old Trafford,
Getting on your nerves.

Wherever you go, wherever you look,
And whatever you do,
He's going to get himself there,
To spoil everybody's view.

Even in Covent Garden,
Watching a magician do his trick,
You can bet that you'll be bothered by,
The prick with the selfie stick.

Pickpockets

City life,
At a pace.
All the same,
Every face.
Push through crowds,
Rush through shops.
Time is precious,
Nothing stops.
Watch the time,
Lots to do.
Meanwhile others,
Watching you.
Crowds around,
Railway station.
Moments loss of,
Concentration.
Quick subliminal,
Distraction.
No time for,
Mental reaction.
Before you can,
Count to one.
Hand slipped in,
The wallets gone.
There's no chance,
To shout out loud.
Disappeared,
Into the crowd.
Just be sure,
Of these trash.
Or they'll have it,
With your cash.

A solitary rose

A solitary rose
Lies across the bed
In the very place
You had laid your head.
Your perfume lingers
In the room
To cut through any
Lonesome gloom.
Last night now seems
So far away
I'm dreaming of
Another day.
So now you've gone
Into the night
And left me here
60 quid light.

Why doesn't the poet get groupies?

He's no discernible talent,
He mainly spends his time,
Just playing around with words,
And trying to make things rhyme.
There doesn't seem much interest,
His confidence is flagging,
He tells tales to impress the girls,
But no one wants to shag him.
Cos poets don't get groupies,
The way that rock stars do,
They tend to be kept at a distance,
Like a potential dose of flu.
His favourite opening line is that,
He once was on the telly,
But he doesn't take them to heaven,
By merely quoting Shelley.
He'd studied Keats and Byron,
Who weren't short of some action,
But all he gave in his poetic world,
Was total dissatisfaction.
You see poets don't get groupies,
And they can't understand the cause,
All they can hope for is an odd smile,
And a gentle round of applause.
There's no one waiting at the bar,
Or outside the stage door,
To help his desperate sex life,
Which by now is looking poor.
So if there's any groupies out there,
With a lust who want to show it,
I'll tell you where you need to be,
Right here with the poet.

Doing my best

Don't put me to the test,
I can't do more than my best,
Just let me get on by,
Your expectations are too high,
I don't know what you are seeing,
I'm no superhuman being,
Encouragement is one thing,
But worry's what it will bring,
It's smothering my leisure,
The constant thought of pressure,
So leave me, let me be,
I'm doing this for me,
And I'm doing pretty well,
As far as I can tell,
So don't expect the sky,
Don't set your sights too high
Don't put me to the test,
I'll always do my very best.

Spaced into space

Heart was racing
Like a bass drum pounding
Strobe lighting
Irregular
Quick-slow
A bead of sweat
That feeling inside
Butterflies?
Adrenalin burst
How fast can that pulse go
Anticipation
Flashing images
Confused, distorted
A mass of colour
Almost psychedelic
Whirling, spinning,
Flying yet still.
Gliding with grace
Spaced into space.

Lady Rose

She knows them all
She's laid with the best
She's given it all away.
She's there at a call
For her there's no rest
It's always work no play.

And everyone knows
Where everyone goes
To Lady Rose.

She's on the street
From dawn to dusk
Wherever there's a need.
A friendly greet
A smell of musk
Another one indeed.

And everyone knows
Where everyone goes
To Lady Rose.

She's got loneliness written on her
face
As she wanders on from place to
place
Considering her fall from grace
Through failings of the human
race.

The gent makes a call
He's working late
That's the way it goes.
But after all
He keeps his date
With Lady Rose.

Everyone knows
Where everyone goes
To Lady Rose.

Everyone goes
To Lady Rose.

She'll never close
Lady Rose.

Only God knows
Lady Rose.

Lady Rose.

A poem for Valentines

You are the worm in my apple
You're the mould on my fruit
You're the slug in my truffle box
You're the stone in my boot.

You're the wasp at my picnic
You're the fly in my butter
You're the floater in the swimming pool
You're the condom in the gutter

You're the uninvited cold caller
You're the migraine in my head
You're the screaming baby on the plane
You're the wet patch on the bed.

You're the empty bog roll holder
You're the spider in my bath
You're the caterpillar on my salad
You're my audience that don't laugh.

You're the Lego under my bare foot
You're the dog turd on the grass
You're the nail in my car tyre
You're a pain in the flaming ass.

Beverley Pilkington

Beverley Pilkington the girl, on the Big D peanuts card,
You were the one that made my teenage years so hard.

You stared across at me in the bar every night,
A perfectly formed nut covered sight.

24 bags of nuts on the card on the shelf,
Frustratingly concealing your bikini clad self.

To feed my nut habit I resorted to steal,
To empty the nut card and see you reveal.

I stared at your image by the pickled eggs,
And felt the shivers run down my legs.

To see you there in all your splendour
The most beautiful ever peanut vendor.

The years obsession caused some friction,
Not to mention a peanut addiction.

Oh Beverley Pilkington more than it seems,
Seller of peanuts maker of dreams.

You were the one, a goddess to me,
A lifetime love affair with you and Big D.

I'm not running away

I'm not running away, I'm being pushed,
I'm not hurrying up, I'm being rushed,
As long as I stay, I'm being crushed,
That's why I'm going.

Things have changed, I stayed the same,
There's now new rules, within the game,
It's only time that is to blame,
That I'm knowing.

No point in staying another hour,
The whole thing's like a crumbling tower,
There's no more tea when the milks turned sour,
The cracks are showing.

I'm not trying to hide, I'm in full view,
I tried to make it work with you,
But the weather changed, and that is true,
There's an ill wind blowing.

And so I'll turn around and make my way,
Have some fond thoughts of yesterday,
But the whistle's gone for the close of play,
There's a new river flowing.

Strolling through

Strolling through the park at midnight
Sees reflections all around

Low lights bringing lengthening shadows
Stalking death won't make a sound

Wind blows through a kind of chilling
Breeze, that says loves not for hire

No deep valleys, darkened alleys
Portals, doorways hide the fire

Meters justice on transgressor
Truth is hammered home again

But one more just like the other
Insidiously plays the game.

Commitment

I'll see you Friday for a fun day
Don't wanna come for tea on Sunday

Just wanna have a sexy summer
Don't wanna go and meet your momma

We can go out whenever you're ready
Don't tell your friends we're going steady

We have a laugh we have a bevvy
Don't want things to get too heavy

Stay over my place when we're grooving
Don't get settled, please don't move in

I like you for the fun you bring
Don't wanna buy a diamond ring

I only want to make you smile
Don't wanna take you down the aisle

I'm happy with you playing my game
But I don't want you taking my name

Let's just keep it the way that this is
Ain't gonna end up Mr and Mrs !

Don't worry, kids

Don't worry about the bogey man cos everybody knows,
He's made up by your parents to keep you on your toes.
Don't worry about ghosts, apparitions and spooks,
Because they aren't real, just in films and in books.
Don't worry about monsters under your bed,
There are none, It's all just in your head.
Don't worry about Dracula, vampires and ghouls,
They come from imagination of fools.
Don't worry about aliens and Daleks from space,
They're just on TV and not at your place.
King Kong and Godzilla, add them to the list,
No problem either, cos they don't exist.
Don't worry about these, they are all just pretenders,
Save your worries for paedophiles and sex offenders!

Tell me

Tell me
Why do you cry my girl
Take your time
Look around
Your world weighs too much for you
Maybe things can never be the same
My love struck dreamer
With the stars in mind
Don't make a fool of yourself
You look so hard you can't see
It's a wilder world than you know
Stay as you are for your good
You don't need others
I'll accompany you in your dreams
I'll guide you through ideals
I haven't slept for many days

Souvenirs

I've got a red tea towel, showing flamenco dance
A set of sea view coasters, from the South of France
I've got a tatty bathrobe, from a Rome hotel
Some reproduction after shave, with a questionable smell
A stuffed donkey from an Alicante store
A ceramic number 3 on my front door
I've got a voodoo doll from New Orleans
From Mexico a bag of jumping beans.

A Rasta hat and dreads, some Carnaby Street threads
A block of Kendal cake, it's not cake for goodness sake!
Some clotted cream from Bude, Greek statue rather rude
A pair of maracas from Spain, a model of an Orient train
A sighing Venetian bridge hanging from my fridge
Bottle of Albanian scotch, a dodgy Rolex watch
A T- shirt cheap and shitty saying, 'I heart New York city'
A Liverpool Beatles mug, a Devon toby jug
A leprechaun for luck, an Eddie Stobart truck
A large 'down under' flag, a Quantus 'chunder bag'
A leaning Pisa tower, Swiss clock that chimes the hour
A palm tree in the shower, a plastic lotus flower
Some plates upon a wall I don't even recall
Coloured sand from Cornwall, things that just mean sod all.

Souvenirs from overseas and Britain too
Tacky reminders of my times with you.

The Cheshire Set

Spacious private leafy lane,
Sun rises over the pool again.
Opulent mansions dot the scene,
Rising from the rolling green.
Ferrari's presence opens gate,
This babe ain't gonna make him late.
Into the city or maybe to train,
Another kick or financial gain.
Then quiet falls the domestic towers,
Just have another couple of hours.
They are up and about at the crack of 11,
Off for the morning coffee shop heaven.
Brunch with the gang, latte and cake,
Ease into the day for goodness sake.
Appointment at 3 at 'Gerard's', for hair,
School run left to the trusty au pair.
There's a free appointment, they're in luck,
Just up the street for a nip and tuck.
In their 4x4's from Alderley Edge,
Off to Waitrose for their fruit and veg.
Avocado, cucumber and yoghurt too,
Fresh mint, lentil and mange tout.
It's not health food to help to make them thin,
They don't eat it, they rub it on the skin.
Then off back home to their high class places,
With designer children and designer faces.
Hubby's back she hears the car,
Greets him with the standard 'mwah.'
Scotch and soda out ready for him,
As she takes her early evening swim.
And round off the evening not too boozy,
Just a bottle of Bollinger in the jacuzzi.
From dawn to dusk it's tough you bet,
Oh the strain of being in the Cheshire Set.

Nothing here

The world we found was sound and round and up its own black hole.

There's far too many shots been missed to hope to find the goal.

As Lucifer's lieutenants busily stoke the coal.

It's time to take the front position adopt the leading role.

As pacifist spectators avoid walking on the grass.

As governments make laws depending on their class.

Insensitive, thoughtless, mindless, the whole case bloody crass.

The working man can't have his say he doesn't have the brass.

So stand up and be discounted, disregarded, left in fear.

Any pointless protests only land on the deaf ear.

It's every man for someone else they couldn't make it clear.

So take your lot and plot as there's nothing for you here.

The King of comedy

With dinner suit and bow tie,
Stomach pointing south,
The working men's club comedian,
All sweat and filthy mouth.

Standing there red faced,
With old jokes ready to crack,
Looking like he's on the brink,
Of a fatal heart attack.

His look has badly dated,
He's not getting any trendier,
Nor endearing himself to audiences,
With his sexist, racist agenda.

The poor guy's still stuck in the 70's,
Stubbornly refusing to adapt,
He's trying in vain for an audience laugh,
And can't remember when they last clapped.

He's a walking anachronism,
Less relevant now than ever,
His art form is way past its sell by date,
Despite his determined endeavour.

So he needs to have a rethink,
And play a different card,
Because him and his act are heading,
For the comedy graveyard.

Travelling Ryanair

You used to use bad airlines but now you think you've got it right,
You're determined not to have the food but then you think you might,
The food is indescribable, no that's not true it's shite.
When you travel on a Ryanair flight.
You queue up for an hour hoping you will board up soon,
But the queue only takes you to a tiny stuffy room,
The whole experience from now is only doom and gloom,
When you travel on a Ryanair flight.
To put up with all this you need the patience of a saint,
The steward will help you if you feel a little faint,
But don't get too close 'cos he has breath that could strip paint,
When you travel on a Ryanair flight.
A dirty grey tracksuit seems the standard thing to wear,
There's no point dressing nicely as nobody will care,
The general chavvy feeling is just too much to bear,
When you travel on a Ryanair flight.
You pick your destination from every place it goes,
Your luggage may go with you too but no one really knows,
The in flight entertainment's when the steward picks his nose,
When you travel on a Ryanair flight.
You quite fancy a nice drink but there's nothing good to sup,
The vinegary wine is served warm in a paper cup,
You have to wait for takeoff, till the pilot sobers up,
When you travel on a Ryanair flight.
The plane is full of British with tender sun burnt bits
Queuing noisily at the toilet as they all have got the shits
If you take a while to look you'll see they're just a set of gits
When you travel on a Ryanair flight.
So why don't you give them a try so that you can see,
If all that I have told you can in fact really be,
And if you're very lucky you'll be sitting next to me,
When you travel on a Ryanair flight.

The morning after the life before

This is the morning after
The life before
That was some party
That was my life
But you called last orders
While I was going strong

This is the morning after
The life before
That was some game
That was my life
But you blew the final whistle
At half time

This is the morning after
The life before
Shakespeare's finest hour
That was my Juliet
But you drew the final curtain
At the interval

And the conversation ended with lots left to say
And the sun came down on my love at midday

........this is the morning after the life before

........this is the morning after the love before.

Life's not fair

When your future is judged by the state of your past,
Your basic upbringing is down to your class,
And a working class lad finds it hard to progress,
As he isn't the guy that will only say yes.
And life's not fair

To the chap on the street who was dealt a bad hand,
And the unlucky type never found in demand,
And is then written off with hardly a thought,
Just because it's the way that these people are taught.
And life's not fair

To the single young mother raising her child,
And her world's chaotic going wild,
Coping with prejudice judgement and hate,
Trying to get by with no help from the state.
And life's not fair

When your children are told what a bad dad you were,
With one sided stories and lies they don't care,
And your decency stops you from pointing the blame,
Or just joining in with a point scoring game.
And life's not fair

If you're considered wrong if too fat or too thin,
Or you don't fit in with your colour of skin,
And religious beliefs are a cause for concern,
Yet general acceptance is all that you yearn.
And life's not fair

When you don't have any say over where you are born,
Where there's drought or famine or land is war torn,
And you just try to live one day at a time,
But each one of those days there's a mountain to climb .

And life's not fair
To animals who have no voice to be heard,
Killed for ivory and skins when gain is the word,
To profit from life of one living being,
With backs firmly turned so no one is seeing.

And life's not fair
When the way you are treated depends on your sex,
You're subject to scrutinous rigorous checks,
The fight to be seen makes you tired and weary,
Equality's an ideal although just in theory.

And life's not fair
When you work 60 hours scrubbing and cleaning,
And sweating all weathers it hardly has meaning,
When you earn just enough to survive what you've got,
Yet a footballer's weekly could buy him a yacht.

And life's not fair
When being a good person doesn't guarantee long life,
And evil survives causing horror and strife,
And the good ones are taken before their time,
And you think religion's no reason or rhyme.

And life's not fair
To the child that can't live a life that's the norm,
Be clouded of mind or twisted of form,
Bringing pain and causing a family torn,
And the poor little thing didn't ask to be born.

And life's not fair
The world is symmetrical from a distance,
And we believe in all's equal existence,
But look a bit harder and soon you discover
As Orwell said 'Some are more equal than others'.
Because life's not fair.

The Carvery

The carvery phenomenon is back
The new way to over feed,
The self service meal approach
An open invitation to greed.

Got to charge through to the buffet
bar
Got to give everything a try,
Get the biggest plate imaginable
And pile it unfeasibly high.

And waddle back to the table
Dripping gravy as they go,
Dropping bits of soggy cabbage
In a trail along the floor.

It's eat all you like, not all you can
Take just what you like to your
table,
It's not an actual challenge
Of eat all that you are physically
able.

Still they carry bucketfuls of grub
Spilling onto the table cloth,
They don't really need a table
They'd be more at home with a
trough.

With an urgency to get more on
the plate
No particular manners on view,
They pile till they can pile no more
I'll bet they fill their pockets too.

So this is it as they dive in
Devouring without any cares,
They've settled down for pigfest
As they strain their bulging chairs.

An Olympic event in the gluttony
games
An art form the way they do,
Known locally as the greed feed
It's an embarrassment to view.

It's as though they've not had a
meal for weeks
Their physique is all heading
south,
My sympathy goes with their sad
affliction
Of only having one mouth !

Guns

Don't like to get political
Analytical
Or be critical
But a country that shuns
Abolition of gun
A system that stuns
That is willing
And instilling
A culture of killing
Should not be surprised
By its own demise
Born of hate, to despise
Focus just on wealth
Ignore mental health
Govern with stealth
A nation
With gun fixation
Begs confrontation
From an armed population
Heading for suffocation
Self termination
And so it's said
With public dread
Innocent till proven dead
So land of the brave
Guns protect and save?
Tell it to the grave !

I want to be a ranting poet

I want to be a ranting poet,
I've got the accent right, I know it,
Aggressive delivery of my own,
And talking in a monotone,
I've got no talent and want to show it,
By being,
A ranting poet.
It's easy when you get the hang,
You don't use big words just slang,
You don't have worries trying to fit,
All the things you want to say on one line because in ranting
poetry it doesn't matter anyway and no one gives a shit.
No one laughs and no one smiles,
At poems that go on for miles,
So how can I make my name,
With poems that all sound the same,
Johnny Clarke did it, he showed the way,
A living legend still today.
I have to think of something new,
And give it my political left wing view,
Talk about things that have happened to me,
Nostalgia's not what it used to be,
Or wars and crime and unemployment,
Dole queues, bus queues
Snooker cues ? Disappointment .
Walking the streets up and down all day,
Depressing everyone going my way,
No this ranting poetry's not for me,
I thing I'll have to leave it be,
I had a go I had my try,
I think I'll sod off home now
Bye .

What's in the news ?

There's an all out strike at the railway station
And the President has upset another nation.
A footballer's been out and up to no good
While a Caribbean island is under a flood.
Another prison breaker is out on the run
Some maniac in U.S. goes crazy with a gun.
While teachers and nurses are still underpaid
And shops throughout the country are struggling for trade.
And parks and playgrounds are closing everyday
And children now have nowhere left to play.
More cuts breaking down the NHS
Waiting lists grow longer the system's a mess.
And Brexit negotiations now seem quite unreal
As Europe won't play ball and cut us a deal.
And there's knife crime and everyone watches their backs
And there's constant reports of acid attacks.
A boat of freedom seekers has capsized in the Med
Their desperate plight has left many dead.
Our athletes still have little hope
As another fails a test for dope.
MP is discovered, dressing in tights
Claiming expenses on cruising red lights.
And accountants confuse by talking in riddles
Concealing their wealthy star clients tax fiddles.
They say male domination's a thing of the past
Not listening to those being sexually harassed.
Don't forget the showbiz romps and affairs
Which Royal has been dating, oh who the fuck cares.
The news is depressing there's no doubt about it
But what would we be doing or saying without it.
The world is diseased of that I am sure
And the sad thing is, we don't look for a cure.

I'm killing the earth single handed

My shampoo is tested in a seals eye,
My deodorant causes holes in the sky,
I deposit carbon footprints as I go by,
I'm killing the earth single handed.

My car sends toxic fumes into the air,
But I carry on driving as though I don't care,
I'm poisoning the atmosphere and I know it ain't fair,
I'm killing the earth single handed.

When I flush the toilet it turns up in the sea,
Then all our children are swimming in wee,
They'll all be sick and it's down to me,
I'm killing the earth single handed.

I love to eat a juicy fresh pork pie,
But it always ends up making me cry,
Cos I'm making the little cute piggies die,
I'm killing the earth single handed.

The natural world is going broke,
My plastic bag for life makes wildlife choke,
It's a bag for death that ain't no joke,
I'm killing the earth single handed.

Global warming is easily felt,
The hand of fate already dealt,
If I turn up my heating the ice caps will melt,
I'm killing the earth single handed.

My leather three piece suite is the furniture from hell,
That's the most un PC thing as far as I can tell,
It's depleting the rain forests and animals as well,
I'm killing the earth single handed.

I just suppose I don't really think,
As I empty chemicals down my sink,
That I'm putting the world out on the brink,
I'm killing the earth single handed.

The pointing finger has finally landed,
The trash pile of the world has expanded,
A polluter is what I am now branded,
I'm killing the earth single handed.

Costanerobucks

'Could I have a coffee please ?'

Do you want a skinnie latte
Or a mocha with some flakes.
Or a black Americano
Goes very well with cakes.
Or maybe a flat white
With milk or some cream.
We could add some vanilla
To make it a dream.
You ain't seen nothing till
you've had a Macchiato
Or sat back chilling with
A fresh made Ristretto
You could try a Mochiato
It's a bit of a mixture.
A baristas cocktail
Would paint a good picture.
Or a steaming Cortado
To satisfy the thirst.
Or maybe Espresso
To give you a burst.
You can't beat Cappuccino
I'm sure you'll agree.
'No, stop!
Just bring me a cup of tea'

'There's earl grey or jasmine
Darjeeling or mint
There's apple that's flavoured
With spice, just a hint
Ceylon orange pekoe or
Red velvet crush
English rose, lychee,
Vanilla honey bush
Just some suggestions,
Of some you might try'
'No thanks mate
I only want the free WiFi'

Wedding

I've got to go to a wedding
One really shouldn't moan
They are usually happy occasions
Except of course your own

The couple look delightful
In front of all the gang
The groom looks like he's in the dock
And the bride like a lemon meringue

As they stand proud at the altar
The front few rows have noticed
The vicar right in front of them
Has dreadful halitosis

When he spits out that immortal line
All are filled with dread
Does anyone know a reason why
These two should not be wed

They worry someone will speak up
But luckily they don't
So they both say yes I do, I will
But we know of course they won't

It's off to the reception
The best part of the day
The hard work now it's over
And so it's time to play

The bride's father looking smart
Downing endless pints of Stella
While the grooms mother with her posh hat
The size of an umbrella

The usher loves a bit of scram
He's tucked in to the food
First at any buffet
Before the crowd ensued

There's aunts and uncles, cousins too
Joining in the fun
Putting on fake grins and smiles
Pretending to get on

The party now is in full swing
Grandmas dancing looks the part
While Grandad slumps in a corner
As usual pissed as a fart

The best man's on a mission
Trying to prove he is the best
He struts his stuff on the dance floor
In boxers and a vest

It's only a matter of time
Before, up goes a shout
And both sides of the family join
As the wedding fight breaks out

It all comes out from the stag night
When he'd told her that he missed her
And all the time he was back at home
Sleeping with her sister

The chairs and tables were flying
Amongst the shouts and cries
The best man caught the bouquet
Right between the eyes

Can we have some order now
The hotel manager begs
As his face becomes the target for
A plate of warm scotch eggs

It's every man for himself
Fortune favours the brave
As the usher dives under the table
With as much buffet as he can save

The lights go on the police are called
It's time the music stops
Uncle Charlie makes a quick exit
As he's wanted by the cops

The sergeant shouts 'you've all to leave
Now go for goodness sake'
And granny says 'well that's a mess
I haven't had me cake'

So everyone dispersed now
The bar has finally closed
What the fuss was all about
No one really knows

But the groom's walking the corridors
Wrapped up in just some bedding
The bride's in tears, necking beers
Another fun family wedding

Its two o'clock in the morning
And so the church bell tolls
As the usher finally emerges
With the last of the sausage rolls

The hotel is now in darkness
To the managers elation
And all look forward to next week
And another great celebration.

You can dam the river

You can dam the river, but you won't stop it flowing,
You can hold me back, but you won't stop me going,
Nothing for us now, not knowing what we're knowing,
The love we tried to nurture long ago stopped growing.

You can ask and ask and carry on repeating,
You can break my heart, but you won't stop it beating,
I'm moving forward certainly not retreating,
There's an honour of lovers that doesn't involve cheating.

You can change your politics any way you are inclined,
You can change opinions but you'll never change my mind,
There's a new future now that's there for me to find,
It was your choice by the way if I need to remind.

I'm really not for turning whatever news you bring,
I'm following my own course just as Summer follows Spring,
I finally get to go and just do my own thing,
Why not do your normal and have another fling.

It won't make any difference however much you're yearning,
You may as well hope that the sun will stop burning,
You taught me the hard way and now I am learning,
There's only one outcome you can't stop my world turning.

Do you ?

Do you look
Where you're going
More than shun
Where you have been
Do you like
What you're seeing
Or ignore
What you've seen
Can you adore
All life's wonders
Live in awe
Of all that's there
Appreciate
the beauty
Or don't
You really care ?

Walking home shameless

Walking home shameless soaked in guilt
Steps over the man with the cardboard box quilt

Through wet cobbled streets the rain is pouring
Every step of the feet, the guilt is soaring

Concocting his story rehearsing his lies
The shame and deceit shine through vacant black eyes

This surreptitious world so far from his home
Idyllic domesticity stripped to the bone

Just Mr. Average, with average dependents
In stained office garb at daybreak resplendent

It's living a lie, it's lying a life
Deceiving himself, his family and wife

Reassuring himself this way is no crime
Fooling no one and there's always next time

Walking home shameless soaked and frozen
Living the lifestyle of which he has chosen.

Where a lot of poets go wrong,

Where a lot of poets go wrong,
Is making their poems too long....

Autumn

A beautiful sunrise defies the cold
The streets now frequented by only the bold.
Deceptive beauty from picturesque Fall
Entices hundreds of artists to call.
Fireball sun blazes through skeletal trees
The last fallen leaves float down in the breeze.
A seasonal farewell as summer will end
And cloak of darkness begins to descend.
Myriad colours of rust red and brown
Autumnal carpet that's lining the ground.
Crisp and crunching under lovers feet
As hand in hand stroll down the street.
Visual breath through cold fresh air
Wrapped in each other they don't care.
Seasons do as seasons will
Whether warm or weather chill.

A Teenagers (My) Bedroom

Roger Dean posters on the wall,
Pile of records from a market stall.
Football books, Goal and Shoots,
Levi jeans and baseball boots.
Poster of lyric to Desiderata,
Remnants of pizza of cheese and tomato.
World peace logo on the door,
Domestic bomb site on the floor.
Half full cups of old cold tea,
Pot noodles scattered randomly.
Tennis girl poses rather cheeky,
Parade magazines hidden, sneaky.
Over chair, school shirt and tie,
Dirty clothes dumped, piled high.
Tie dye shirts, flares and loons,
Gramophone plays groovy tunes.
All the favourites yet again,
Life on Mars, Virginia Plain.
Fashion shots with Steed and Tara,
Trendy T shirt, Che Guevara.
Programmes from the Man United,
Best, Law, Charlton, so excited.
Huge great pile of NME's,
Carpet trodden Dairyleas.
A teenager's bedroom, his world's centre,
Beware to those who brave to enter.

Changes

Got stubble on my chin
Got dirt on my face
Not slept for a week
I look a disgrace
I've black finger nails
And feel like hell
I'm emitting a pretty
Nauseating smell
I'm wandering around
Along the street
Weary body
And aching feet
The neglect reflects on
The state of my breath
Pungent repellent and
Stinking of death
I'm going round bars
Drinking the dregs
Feeling my underwear
Stick to my legs
My hair is greasy
Dank and long
With quite an exclusive
And interesting pong
I won't stay like this
I'll turn my life round
I'll get a real job
I'll think more profound
Then there'll come the days
When I will feel prudent.
And no longer live
This life as a student

The following poems are all on a theme,
that being my favourite city, Manchester.

On the Metro Link

Get on the tram
Don't smile, be cool
This way is the
Unwritten rule.
Stare into space
It's right it's fact
The rule says no
Social interact.
Don't look don't speak
Just walk on by
No idle chat
No eye to eye.
Won't be long
Until your station
Still avoiding
Conversation.
Keep to yourself
Just do not look
Do a crossword
Read a book.
Headphones on
Stay alone

Only talk is
On the phone.
If you connect
Could be the end
They may want to
Be your friend.
So look away
Get out of it
Just remember
You're a Brit.
Brits don't mix
Brits don't mingle
That's not cricket
Just stay single
So on the tram
Head down low
Worry not for
They'll all go.
All that way
No conversation
Well done, here's
Your destination.

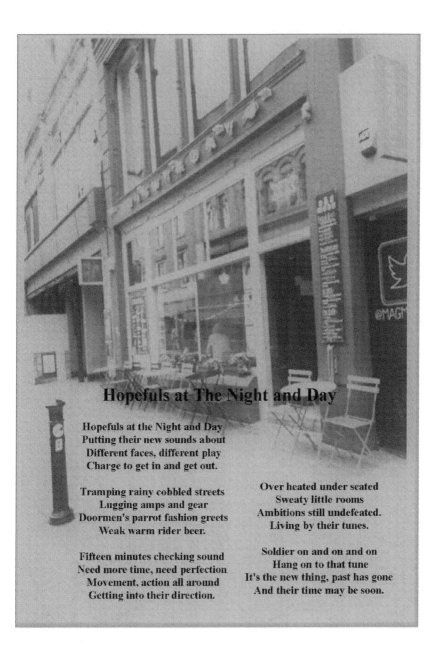

Hopefuls at The Night and Day

Hopefuls at the Night and Day
Putting their new sounds about
Different faces, different play
Charge to get in and get out.

Tramping rainy cobbled streets
Lugging amps and gear
Doormen's parrot fashion greets
Weak warm rider beer.

Fifteen minutes checking sound
Need more time, need perfection
Movement, action all around
Getting into their direction.

Over heated under seated
Sweaty little rooms
Ambitions still undefeated.
Living by their tunes.

Soldier on and on and on
Hang on to that tune
It's the new thing, past has gone
And their time may be soon.

70's Manchester.

Wednesday morning at school was double history
Why people attended was a complete mystery
So.....

I was off to Manchester on the train
Checking out the scene in the pouring rain
Jumping on the train at Bolton street station
Arrival in Victoria quite an elation
Dodging the traffic to Market Street market
To check out the latest gear was our target
Spending spree for less than a fiver
Hanging round Justins and Stolen from Ivor
Loons and tank tops Ben Sherman too
Two toned pants and platform shoes
Budgie jackets keep the 'Faith'
Harrington jacket bit more safe
Oblivious to my fabulous flares
The street market traders arranging their wares
Costermongers shouting their produce
Gift of the gab is sure put to good use
Off to the cool corporation street cafe
Pies and milk shakes fag and a laugh
A great big juke box stood at the door
Loaded with Roxy and Bowie and Quo
Hunting for vinyl shops, had to do
Hime and Addison, Rare Records too
Queuing for tickets avoiding the bouncer
Getting your bootlegs from under the counter
Wander up Tib street where anything goes
All is for sale and everyone knows

Characters on every street that you walk
Reflecting sadness on the roads that they stalk
The grey haired lady looking chilly
Feeding the pigeons in Piccadilly
So close to the fraught street living guys
Risking another night under the skies
A city on the up ever developing
Tower blocks from all sides enveloping
Glitzy, flash hotels, nothing bland
Stars at the Portland, Midland and Grand
Diversive, divisive, easy to take you
Supportive, derisive, equally make you
Loving every moment for all that I'm worth
Manchester centre, the heart of the earth.

Great Ducie Street

Looking for new gear,
The latest lines are here,
All the names, no fear,
On Great Ducie Street.

In the shadow of Strangeway's tower,
You can shop at any hour,
Anarchy empowered,
Down on Great Ducie Street.

Shopping for some flash,
No wasting cash on trash,
You know just where to dash,
Great Ducie Street.

For fashion in the style,
The prices make you smile,
Walk the bargain mile,
Of Great Ducie Street.

Standing on the brink,
They know what you think,
Tip the man the wink,
Down on Great Ducie Street.

Label says Milan,
Invoice says Taiwan,
Get it while you can,
On Great Ducie Street.

Directions furtive muttered,
Shelves of stock are cluttered,
Shop fronts all are shuttered,
Down Great Ducie Street.

Patrol car slowly goes,
And everybody knows,
Doors kept safely closed,
Down Great Ducie Street.

As livings there are earned,
Street life lessons learned,
Blind eyes firmly turned,
On Great Ducie Street.

The meet and greet
It's neat and sweet
There's no receipt
Can't beat the treat
It's all discreet
Where they secrete
Their retail retreat
On Great Ducie Street

The laws elite
Are on their feet
Cops on the beat
Turn up the heat
But can't compete
And know they're beat
Sweet in defeat
On Great Ducie street

In the Northern Quarter of Manchester.........

An eclectic mix of restaurants and bars
From pretty much every nation.
There's Russian, Arab, Moroccan or French
And a Chippy near Victoria station.

There's street food on every corner
The corners of every street
If you want some Jamaican jerk chicken
You're in for a Caribbean treat.

Hipsters hang out at the cafe bars
Slung back in an antique armchair
With a caramel latte and cinnamon bun
With their beards and designer hair.

Art exhibitions and galleries galore
Auctions on which you can bid.
Splash out on a limited edition print
Or a postcard for 20 quid !

There are shops that sell vinyl records
They play with a needle or 'stylus'
They're often full of crackles
Like the pirates played on the wireless.

The famous Afflecks Palace
Can keep you amused for hours
Whether you're Mod or Emo or Goth
Or hippy - all oil and flowers.

There are specialist shops for all tastes
Everything that you could hope
From a fragrant smelling bath bomb
To a seven inch cock on a rope.

There's a genuine Banksy painting
That's only partly on show
Cos it's half covered up with graffiti
Ironic, I know !

It's the best place for current live music
In bars on every street
Places you'll stick to the carpet
And on the way out wipe your feet.

Cocktails with their herbs and spices
Priced up however they feel
A small Daiquiri or a Mojito
For the price of a three course meal.

Retro fashions everywhere
50's bumpers on the feet
And right on cue outside the door
A tram on the cobbled street.

Ubiquitous buskers will entertain
With songs from the near and the far
With a McDonalds coffee cup full of small change
And a battered acoustic guitar.

Performance poets regale their prose
With lines of grief and humour
A lot of them wordsmiths with clever rhymes
But some not so good ....

The Northern Quarter of Manchester
Is a unique and fabulous place
You'll leave a good few quid lighter
With a wonderful smile on your face.

The following three poems were written after the terrorist
attack at the Manchester arena.
The first one on the day after, the second the following bank
holiday and the third one a year on.

Mancs – a City United.

They can't shake us,
Or try to remake us,
They won't take us,
Or ever break us.
This one great community,
Always in total unity,
They can't pull apart,
A Manchester heart,
That pumps inside,
With local pride,
They'll never intimidate,
With actions fuelled by hate,
This resolve of so long,
A City United so strong,
We're a kind that bind,
With each other and find,
That strength within,
Will beat evil sin,
From the despicable weak,
Who can only seek,
And aim if they could
To destroy what is good
With no courage just shame,
In NO God's name,
And together we stand,
With strength hand in hand,
Always side by side,
Will never divide.
........Mancs.

29/05/17

Spent today in the heart of a hurt, fractured city,
Whose people stood solid and needed no pity.

Thousands are gathered in the square in near silence,
Reflecting the outcome of hatred and violence.

While children of wide ethnic range play together,
Running through fountains in bank holiday weather.

And smiling at each other as the parents watch with pride,
A multi cultural gathering where no one has to hide.

Their thoughts and beliefs that come from above,
Manifest in purity, innocence and love.

It's a beautiful sight but not sure if it should,
Take evil to bring out this bounty of good.

Never forget

When hardships come
And all can help
Support and aid are there.
And all are one
And love shines through
And everyone will care.

The world will watch
And grieve along
Help endure the time.
But time moves on
And priorities
Are often redefined.

So months go by
And flowers cleared
As people come and go.
And little more
Is left to tell
Nothing now to show.

But still the lives
And still the loss
And still the tears and pain.
And still the image
Clearly there
Forever will remain.

Never forget.

And finally ....

The nostalgia section.

A few poems relating to
memories of my
childhood and
the places where
I lived and grew up.

Mitchell Street

Running up Mitchell Street cobbles
After school, my grandad and me
A race to get home to a roaring fire
And Grandad making our tea.

Mum and dad got home much later
They both worked at factories nearby
And when they got in we'd all sit together
And tuck into Grandad's meat pie.

There were twenty houses on our street
All facing a big factory wall
And we'd play every night until dark
On our bikes or kicking a ball.

There wasn't much on the streets back then
So it was safe to play out there alone
There were only two houses had cars at that time
And only one house with a phone.

My school was just at the end of our block
That suited me just fine
Cos every morning I didn't set off
Till the clock said one minute to nine.

There was plenty to do after school
I'd go out with my mate and his dogs
We'd go looking around in the nearby ponds
For newts and tadpoles and frogs.

In summer we'd be out on the fields
For hours on end playing cricket
With a bat and a ball that I got off my dad
And an oil drum we used as a wicket.

As time went on things changed
And we changed somewhat too
No cricket or football after school now
We had much better things to do.

There was fashion and music and youth clubs
Buying records and playing them loud
Going out in your flares and Ben Sherman shirt
Trying to stand out from the crowd.

Wednesday's and Friday's at Elton Youth Club
Smoking and having a dance
Chatting to any girl that would listen
While trying to find some romance.

The lad who looked the oldest
Would get us some booze from the pub
And we'd all sit around in a gang with the girls
In the dark at the back of the club.

I went back to that Mitchell Street house
And everything had changed
There were two cars outside every door
And the factory was all rearranged.

Every one now had telephones
And dishes out on the wall
It wasn't safe to ride a bike
And no one played out at all.

The park was locked up and no one could play
No balls being kicked around
And on the corner to break my heart
The youth club had been knocked down.

Black and white images transform into colour
As new buildings replace all the old
And memories play lots of tricks with the mind
And those endless hot summers now seemed cold.

Hang on to your childhood memories
Cos things tend to change too fast
And always remember the fun that you had
Cos they'll take away your past.

They were times that were fondly remembered
And always bring a tear to the eye
And if I close my eyes and think really hard
I can still smell Grandad's meat pie.

I remember when....

Your phone was in a box at the end of the street,
We'd chips and scraps on Fridays as a special treat.
When policemen on the beat looked so much older,
The dustman on the street carried bins on his shoulder.
Rag and bone man would call with his horse and cart,
And the horse would leave a present as it did depart.
When the pop man delivered direct to our door,
No supermarkets then, just the local store.
Our little bit of pocket money would quickly vanish,
With a quarter of rainbow kali and a couple of hard Spanish.
We would go to the local sweet shop that had a vast array,
Shrimps, white mice and chocolate logs on the penny tray.
Opal Fruits and Spangles, Aztec bars were neat,
Fry's Five Centre, Spanish Gold and crunchy Peanut Treats.
There were shops at the end of nearly every street,
You didn't use a car you always used your feet.
Cars were a luxury that few could afford,
There was nothing laid on but we never got bored.
We were told to get out make our own fun and play,
And we did, on our own, or with mates every day.
Always wanted to play out happily whenever,
Didn't mind the time of day, didn't mind the weather.
Make a 'bogey' from planks and old pram wheels,
Didn't have any brakes just dug in our heels.
We'd go out for conkers and climb big trees,
And come home with cuts and badly grazed knees.
We'd save our bus fare for sweets, and walk to our school,
Having a laugh on the way and playing the fool.
We gargled with TCP and rubbed Vic on our chest,
And went to school in a ragged string vest.
And the nit nurse would come round and root through our hair,
To be absolutely sure that no crawlies were there.
We had injections for diseases that put us in tears,
With a scar that was left for 40 odd years.

To stop us from dying from what? They were vague,
Probably Scurvy, Black Death and Plague.
Our house was a terrace, they all looked the same,
Industrial revolution they said was to blame.
We'd an outside toilet with paper on the floor,
And a dark dirty coal shed right next door.
So you'd sit on a cold seat in winter out the back,
Surrounded by spiders and sacks of nutty slack.
There were torn up newspapers put there by me mum,
And we'd leave the toilet with newsprint on our bum.
You could put a pot under your bed but you got no warning,
That the whole bloody room would stink in the morning.
We did washing up in the same sink that I had my nightly wash,
We'd a rubber tap mixer which I thought was quite posh.
There was a tin bath set out in front of the fire,
A few kettles of water were all we required.
We had a record player that was mainly used by me,
Mum got it me for Christmas on t'drip you know, HP.
One Christmas I asked for a drink from the boozy tray,
I drank 2 glasses of snowball and was sick all Boxing Day.
If the local Bobby ever caught you sneaking a beer,
He'd send you back home with a clip round the ear.
Occasionally during the year the fair would come to town,
And we'd spend a good few hours for only half a crown.
Around the waltzers, speedway and side stalls we would roam,
And end by up taking a half dead goldfish home.
There were power cuts and three day weeks disruption, fear and strikes,
But did we give a fig no sir with space hopper and chopper bikes.
Girls were playing hopscotch or roller skating in school yard,
While boys were playing football, or strutting round acting hard.
We'd no computers, or phones, DVDs or Play Station,
But what we had in abundance was a great imagination.
Tell today's kids all of this and jeer and laugh they might,
But we called them the good old days and ......
............I think that we were right.

Bonfire night. 1960s

'Are ya comin collecting 'bommy wood,'
Said my mate from down the street,
It's only 4 weeks to go now,
And we want to seriously compete.
The street with the biggest bonfire,
Was the pride of all around,
So our parents cleared a big area,
On a patch of unused ground.
We'd go collecting door to door,
At every chance we got,
We'd broken doors and chairs and boxes,
Even a baby's cot.
We'd ask at shops and factories,
Take all their wooden trash,
We'd rip open old settees,
And look for long lost cash.
We'd take anything they give,
Nothing was refused,
We'd end up with splinters in our hands,
And old nails through our shoes.
So when we built our bonfire,
We'd build a den inside,
And the weeks before the big day,
It was our special place to hide.
The wood was piled high and plenty,
With pallets from the local mill,
We gazed at our mighty construction,
With more than a little thrill.

And so the day finally comes,
November 5th is here,
Check the den is empty,
And everyone is clear.
As the dads with bottles of paraffin,
Soak the pile of wood,
Dirty little smiling faces knowing,
This is going to be good.
We tuck into hot black peas,
Treacle toffee, Parkin too,
It's the real taste of bonfire night,
And takes all night to chew.
Dad chucks a match and whoosh it's up,
The flames are climbing high,
I crook my neck and see the bonfire,
Lighting up the sky.
The excitement now immense,
Anticipation uncontrolled,
In wellies gloves and duffle coat,
To keep away the cold.
We'd open up our firework tins,
Watch the rockets fly,
Write our name with sparklers,
In the winter sky.
So all the hours collecting,
Has finally ended here,
At our amazing bonfire on,
The best day of the year.

I don't wanna be old

Standing on the terraces, Saturday at Gigg lane
Cheering on The Shakers in the pouring rain
Shrugging off the winter weather, shaking off the cold
Happy to always be doing all this
I don't wanna be old
Nights out at the youth club snooker with my mates
Sneaky dance to Marvin Gaye, trying to get a date
Walk a girl home hand in hand, feels so good to hold
That hasn't happened for a long long time
I don't wanna be old
Break time in the schoolyard tell the latest joke
With friends behind the bike sheds having a cheeky smoke
Chatting up Suzy Gee and trying to be bold
There won't be many more chances
I don't wanna be old
Being a child only lasts so long, now I have one of my own
She's beautiful in every way so I really shouldn't moan
Even though I love to watch her exciting life unfold
It's getting to me now
I don't wanna be old
Take her off every day and drop her at school gate
Back again at 3.30 excited with the wait
See her smiling face with hands out for me to hold
It's becoming distant memories
I don't wanna be old
Now I walk from one room to another in my central heated flat
What I went there for in the first place, I can't remember that
Or anything else for that matter, or so I'm often told
Too late to do anything about it now
I didn't wanna be old.
The clock can't turn back all those years, the chance of that is slim
I'm clinging on to memories, the future's looking grim
I'm hanging on to every day before I kick the bucket
I may not want to get old but we all do so .... fuck it. !

Ramsbottom

Deep into the Lancashire moors
One small village opens its doors
In the shadow of Peel Tower
A reminder of old northern power
River flowing wide and fast
Tracking the industrial past
Converted mills and cobbled alley
Terraced housing lines the valley
Something here for every taste
Smiles on every vendors face
From early sunrise until dark
There's drivers trying hard to park
There's double lines restricting cars
There's single lines in dubious bars!
Nightlife, fright life, yours to choose
Noisy disco or wine bar schmooze
In the morning market trading
Thoughts of last night now are
fading
Fresh fish, flowers, cakes and pies
Every stall, a great surprise.
Countless Deli's meats and cheeses
Exotic produce always pleases
Restaurants with every dish
Cantonese, vegan, to chips and fish
Italian, Indian, Bangladesh
Turkish, Spanish, anyone's guess
Steam train bringing in the tourists
Car boot shoppers and Railway
purists

Every Sunday comes alive
Thriving village 9 to 5
In the churchyard poor old fella
Parks himself with can of Stella
Oblivious to the bustling town
Middle class affluence all around.
Check out antiques and local
galleries
Should account for chunk of your
salaries
Festivals of music, chocolate and pie
Throwing black puddings will open
your eyes
There's nothing sleepy about this
little place
It's fun and it's culture, but not in
your face
In all of the county the jewel in the
crown
Is no curry house,
It's Ramsbottom town.

My Bolton

Hey look old Leons cafe's closed
Most of the street has been bulldozed
And the pub on the corner that I frequently used
For my student days training on the booze
That homely place where I loved to stay
It's now a fast food takeaway
There's no crowd sound at the football ground
Where Burnden legends could be found
They long since had to blow full time
On this happy childhood place of mine
The home of 'Sir Nat' and great football stars
Is now covered in shopping trolleys and cars

All the once familiar places
Now a host of different faces
Few old buildings now remain
Only street names stay the same
All the factory chimneys high
Our Fred dropped them from the sky
The college where I learned life's tricks
Now just several piles of bricks
The cinema I got my first kiss
Another place that I so miss
The Clarence and the Trotters pubs
The Palais and the Nocturne clubs
They've all gone a similar way
There's empty spaces there today
But life goes on its just progression
To do what's needed no concessions
They say our lives are better now
........I wonder how?

Carr's pasties

It's a culinary institution
Like Warburton's sliced bread
A way of life in Bolton
Gets the population fed.

Beware of cheap imitations
The many pie based nasty's
There's nothing else can touch
The legendary Carr's pasties.

A town with great traditions
Of showbiz sport and food
A leading light of Lancashire
Its glory to be viewed.

See the statue of Fred standing proud
Just down from the mighty town hall
The fabulous Octagon theatre
That has seen great stars one and all.

There's the Market place shopping centre
Where discerning will shop a la mode
But you can't beat the famous Carr's bakery
Standing proud on Manchester road

People travel for miles up to Bolton
Just to walk through that bakery door
And sample delights of great pasties
Pies, sausage rolls and lots more

So if you've not tried yet you really must soon
It's where all the gastronomes meet
Get yourself up to Carr's today
Or you're missing a wonderful treat.

Blackpool

North of Liverpool, West of Manchester,
There's a delightful town on the coast.
It goes by the name of Blackpool,
And really has the most.
You'll love it just for what it is,
It's northern and it's gritty.
And from some certain angles,
Can appear quite pretty,

Because there's...........

Toffee apples, candy thrills,
Sticks of rock and dental bills.
Doughnuts fried in year old fat
Endless shops with endless tat.
Fingered fudge and sticky cakes,
Shop for all designer fakes.
Leather bags all black and tan,
Gucci direct from Taiwan.
Amusement arcades penny pushing
Kids anticipation gushing.
Bingo goers leave the sand,
Blue rinses done, dabbers in hand.
Saucy postcards, carry on laughs,
End of pier photographs.
Pleasure beach rides queue for miles,
Happy kids with beaming smiles.
Roller coasters, donkey rides,
Carousels and water slides.
Off the beach and hustle and bustle,
Roberts oysters, cockles and mussels.
Alan Bradley blood stained trams,
15 year olds pushing prams.

Fish and chips and chips and fish,
Blackpool's ubiquitous dish.
Standing mighty Blackpool tower,
Under constant Blackpool showers.
Endless pubs with dazzling lights,
Stags and hens horrific sights.
Under piers couples courting,
Murky waves with odd things floating.
Golden mile all looking good,
Breaking waves and churning mud.
Mr Whippy on the sand,
Endless ice creams close at hand
Ripleys, Tussauds, Sea Life sharks,
Winter Gardens, Stanley Park.
Go there time and time again,
Perfect shelter from the rain.
5 miles of illuminations,
Glowing celebrity sensations.
Old time favourites light the way,
Frank Sinatra, Doris Day.
In the car along the lights,
Thinking this may take all night.
Slowly passing same, old shop,
Travelling at the speed of stop.
Meanwhile at the B & B,
Lovingly preparing tea.
Seaside landlady cooks at the hob,
Toad in the hole and fag in the gob.

For food and the weather Blackpool's a winner,
There's wind in your hair and there's hair in your dinner.

Bury

We're in no one's shadow, an entity of our own,
From sweat and honest graft our community has grown.
Relationships, marriages, liaisons and unions,
Producing generations of strong Burmunians.
Images from a bygone time standing tall with pride,
The fine imposing Parish Church with old Two Tubs beside.
The site of the old castle that gave the town its name,
Watched over by Sir Robert Peel, all that now remains.
In the heart of industrial revolution,
With Kay's flying shuttle the so called solution.
A landscape of terraces factories and mills,
Sky scraping chimneys and smoke in the hills.
Surrounded by green fields cut through by rivers,
The Roch and the Irwell the main power givers.
Much has changed now to the place that we hold dear,
A return to the tram and a nod to yesteryear.
The people still head up this way time and time again,
To see what Bury offers and it isn't only rain !
A great famous market that brings in the crowds,
With plenty to cheer up and cut through those clouds.
It's a town with huge talent in all of the arts,
Ability and proficiency abound in these parts.
From Olympian medallists and football record makers,
To film and TV actors and blockbuster Oscar takers.
Innovators of industry and award winning musicians,
History's great inventors, government leaders and politicians.
These and many more people bring so much to this town,
Showing true Bury spirit that takes nowt lying down.
We are proud of what we have our movers and our Shakers,
A town of forward thinkers and opportunity takers.
Bury born and Bury bred will always be the same,
With Bury Black Pudding probably running through the veins.

At a gig that I was honoured to do
with the legend, John Cooper Clarke.

Where it all started at 'Laughingas Comedy Clubs' with
Bob Williamson, Bernard Wrigley, Phil Cool and Peter Kay.

Reviews / comments

There is a LOT to enjoy and reflect upon in Steven's collection of poems. He seems to have covered just about everything that most people can relate to, laugh at or fear - from the crap on our televisions to preferring to go to North Korea than IKEA; from idiosyncratic British towns with VERY rude names to being unfortunately related to a traffic warden; from the merits of being insignificant to the annoying proliferation of the ubiquitous selfie stick.

Not much escapes his eagle eye and skilful poetic wit – Ryanair; childhood memories; stupid holiday souvenirs; fish and chips; the bland uniformity that blights our towns – you name it he's probably versified about it.

There are also some moving poems about the Manchester arena bombing and some fine tributes to our lovely northern towns.

This book will make you think and make you laugh. I'm pleased to own it and recommend it!

Dave Dutton –(actor, writer, comic, Lancashire lad).

....'Poetry 'Taylor made' for real people, insightful and delightful'.
John Fleming (Blogger, TV producer, comedy guru).

I love reading the poems Steven writes. every single one either makes me laugh out loud, evokes a memory or poses an interesting question. Often a combination of all the above and more besides to be fair!

Lyndsay Hopkinson (musician, promoter)

'He takes the everyday and makes it personal and makes you smile'
BBC Radio Lancashire.

'It is always a pleasure to welcome Steven to Bacup Folk Club. His poetry is poignant. funny and always well received. He has a lovely way of viewing the world, with an eye for the real and uniquely absurd. He conveys this in his own inimitable style with rhythm, feeling and integrity'.
Dom Dudill Bacup Folk Club.